Princess Victoria and the Prince of Wales, Queen Victoria's eldest children.

STAFFORDSHIRE FIGURES
of the nineteenth century

Amoret and Christopher Scott

Shire Publications Ltd

CONTENTS

Set in 9 point Times roman and printed in Great Britain by C. I. Thomas & Sons (Haverfordwest) Ltd, Press Buildings, Merlins Bridge, Haverfordwest, Dyfed.

British Library Cataloguing in Publication Data available.

ACKNOWLEDGEMENTS
Illustrations on the following pages are acknowledged to: the Brighton Museum and Art Gallery, the Willett Collection, pages 1, 4, 9 (right), 11 (left), 12 (lower), 13 (left), 15, 16, 17, 18, 19 (lower), 29; the Stoke-on-Trent City Museum and Art Gallery, pages 10, 11 (right), 13 (right), 14 (all except lower left), 19 (upper), 20, 21, 22, 23, 24, 26, 27, 28. Others are from the authors' collection. The publishers wish to acknowledge the assistance of Mrs P. A. Halfpenny, Keeper of Ceramics at the Stoke-on-Trent City Museum and Art Gallery, in preparing this Album.

COVER: *Florence Nightingale with a wounded soldier, one of the many figures produced during the Crimean War.*
BELOW: *Queen Charlotte. A portrait plaque, probably made for those unable to afford paintings. These were the forerunners of the later three-dimensional figures.*

A group of small anonymous figures. The two vividly coloured penholders of a parrot and a whippet would have made an attractive addition to a lady's writing desk. The child and dog feature the essential spillholder which appeared in various guises near every fireplace.

EARLY STAFFORDSHIRE FIGURES

The Staffordshire figures covered in this book are, with a few exceptions, the named figures of contemporary characters made between about 1840 and the end of the nineteenth century. To put the group into perspective, the Astbury, Whieldon, Wood and Sherratt figures which preceded them are briefly described in this chapter.

Potters make their pieces in two main ways: by hand, so that every piece is different, or by making a mould so that any number of identical pieces can be made. The earlier Staffordshire figures were basically press moulded with hand-made additions; the later ones (particularly the 'flatbacks') were simply moulded.

Glazing is the process of putting a shiny, waterproof coating on the pottery. Most glazes are simply melted glass and differently coloured glazes were made by adding pigments to the molten glass. Salt-glazing is a hard, shiny covering produced on pottery when a handful of salt is thrown into the kiln while the pots are being baked. The surface of a salt-glazed piece looks rather like orange peel. The process was used in Germany at least as early as the fifteenth century and was introduced in England and patented in 1672.

Some of the earliest figures in clay were the stoneware products made in the early eighteenth century; stoneware was then a new invention and the hard, dense material was a triumph for the Staffordshire potters — particularly when they learnt how to salt-glaze it. Famous products from about 1740 are the 'Pew' and 'Arbour' groups; they are always in plain white (actually rather greyish) stoneware, undecorated, and crudely executed. They take their name from the typical groups of two or three people sitting in a high-backed pew or a pair of lovers under a tree. They are naive, charming and very rare; most of them are in museums. Also from this period are some fine (though almost equally naive) horsemen in the same material.

A parallel development in Staffordshire was the making of earthenware figures from coloured clays, or combinations of clays and coloured glazes. These fall into three groups, which are named after the potters who are thought to have been mainly responsible for them. First

3

Polito's Menagerie, a model of a well known travelling show made about 1830, is one of the most famous Sherratt models. The group has musicians, a hurdy-gurdy player and customers on the stage, under a coloured representation of the animals inside.

are the Astbury figures, in cream, red or brown clay splashed with a few touches of other colours, and covered with a thick, transparent, yellowish glaze. Most are of strange little musicians about 6 inches (150 mm) high with boot-button eyes and supports formed for them as part of the modelling of the clay. Most were press moulded with hand-made additions.

The Astbury figures were followed by the Whieldon type. Thomas Whieldon (1719-95) was one of the most successful potters Staffordshire has produced. His figures were characterised by the use of 'tortoiseshell' glazes on white clay.

Browns and yellows predominate, with blues and greens also used quite extensively. He also made many anonymous figures of soldiers and others, particularly on horseback, and he was fond too of the Chinese-style figures popular at the time.

Whieldon was in business between about 1740 and 1783 and produced very fine earthenwares. Next there came a group of potters, mainly of the Wood family of Burslem, who brought the art of figure making to a high level. From this stage until the named Staffordshire figures of the Victorian era the potters were trying to imitate the qualities and appearance of porcelain. Countless other potters throughout Europe had also been trying to find the secret of porcelain manufacture to compete with the Chinese.

The first of the Wood family were Ralph I (1715-72) and his brother Aaron. The business produced a series of very finely modelled figures with coloured glazes and also a large range of Toby jugs; these early examples of the Toby jug are eagerly sought after. (Toby jugs are so called after 'Toby Philpot', the subject of a popular song published in 1761. The original of Toby Philpot was a famous toper of the day named Harry Elwes.) The most important figuremaker of the family was John, the son of Ralph I. He was in business from about 1777 until 1797 and the business continued under John II until 1830. Ralph Wood's other son, Ralph II, was in business from 1789 to 1795 and was responsible for producing busts, including portraits of Handel and Pope and a wide range of other figures, amongst them classical subjects. His son Ralph III lived for only

twenty-seven years, dying in 1801. Enoch Wood (1759-1840) was the son of Aaron. His output was considerable and varies from the rather stilted subjects beloved of that sentimental age ('Fortitude', for example) to excellent portraits from life, such as his bust of John Wesley modelled in 1781.

Important ancestors of the Victorian Staffordshire chimney ornament were the so-called Sherratt figures. Bull-baiting groups, with a fierce bull set upon by dogs, were a favourite subject; so were domestic scenes with the emphasis on the effects of drink. One of the most famous Sherratt products is a large and complicated model of the entrance to 'Polito's Menagerie'.

The name of Felix Pratt is given to a type of figure characterised by an unmistakable range of colours used for decoration (a treacly orange, dull blue, purply brown, olive green and pale yellow), which were painted under the glaze. These figures were made between 1780 and 1840.

Spaniel-type dogs are among the most popular of all Staffordshire chimney ornaments. They were originally made in pairs in a great variety of size and colour; individual dogs can be found comparatively cheaply although collectors should beware of the many modern reproductions.

A boy with a dolphin, two fishergirls and the Prince of Wales clasping his model yacht.

VICTORIAN STAFFORDSHIRE FIGURES

While the more sophisticated potters were trying to imitate porcelain, Staffordshire figure making deteriorated. But about the time that Queen Victoria came to the throne in 1837, a new generation of potters began to produce unsophisticated, genuinely appealing figures that did not try to disguise the qualities of the clay they were made from and which were designed for a mass market. These Staffordshire figures, whatever the price one may be asked to pay for them today, were made for the man in the street, and particularly the man in the country cottage. The market and the output were carefully matched, as a look at the range of subjects will show.

The Victorian country cottager tended to be fervently patriotic, sentimental, a nonconformist in religion and a great lover of animals, particularly dogs. He scarcely read at all, even if he had learned to. He relied upon word of mouth or example for his news and live presentation for his occasional entertainment. So the immense output of Staffordshire figures gave him royalty and military heroes for his patriotism, lovers and folk heroes for his sentimentality, divines such as John Wesley for his nonconformity, and numerous delightful dogs to put on his chimney-piece. They even kept him abreast of current affairs and politics, particularly when there was something sensational to record. The result is that today these figures provide a unique chronicle of an age full of incident and romance, an age which included royal births, marriages and occasions by the score, glorious victories and defeats almost as stirring, heroes and heroines to make every heart swell with the pride of being an Englishman, and the usual quota of pioneers, rogues and misfits.

So far as it is possible to generalise, the production of Staffordshire portrait figures falls into fairly well defined categories, which are a help in dating: **1840-1845.** Figures were small, richly coloured (usually back and front), complicated so far as the potting is concerned, and notably poor likenesses of the people they were meant to represent. By far the most popular subjects in this period were Queen Victoria and her succession of children.

1846-1855. There were many portraits of the royal children in this decade, notably of the Prince of Wales in a sailor suit. It was the main period of notable civilians, including politicians.

1854-1859. Figures were almost exclusively concerned with the Crimean War (1854-6). Not only British soldiers (and notable figures such as Florence Nightingale) were produced, but also all the allied monarchs. The Indian Mutiny (1857-9) is recorded by a very few figures.

1858-1864. The royal children were getting engaged or married. There was emphasis on American subjects arising from the Civil War and *Uncle Tom's Cabin*.

1865-1880. The main foreign event was the Franco-Prussian War of 1870. Many politicians, criminals, sportsmen and entertainers were commemorated. Both the potting and the decoration became much simpler and the backs of most of the figures were unmodelled and completely undecorated. One of the characteristic colours used in decoration, deep underglaze blue, ceased to be used. The decorators from now on often left the figures almost entirely white, with perhaps a few areas of underglaze black for hair and shoes, a little pink for the cheeks, and an indiscriminate use of gilding. The only vivid colour that remained on the palette was orange.

1880-1902. War was the principal interest during this period, including the Egyptian wars of 1882-5, during which Gordon was murdered at Khartoum, the River War (1896-8) and the South African War of 1899-1902.

There were one or two strange omissions from the gallery of figures. Among writers, Dickens, whose stories gripped the whole nation, is missing and no figure has been found of Lord Palmerston.

By the end of the nineteenth century the Staffordshire figure was dead, overtaken by a variety of factors such as the development of photography, improved education and literacy. Production continued in the old moulds, but the portrait

A group of figures from the period 1865-1880 when the pottery was left white and decorated with a minimum of gilt and black. These uncoloured models are less popular and therefore cheaper than the brightly coloured groups. The central figures stand on either side of a 'pocket' in which a watch could be inserted.

figure as part of an unsophisticated chronicle of contemporary events was no more.

It is not easy to say who made Victorian Staffordshire figures. While the earlier figures were classified under the name of the best known potter in a particular style, such as Sherratt or Astbury, the output of the Staffordshire potteries in the nineteenth century was so widespread and enormous that even this loose kind of classification is difficult. Hardly any of the figures are marked: copyright was not worth enforcing for pieces that sold for a few shillings and any successful figure was pirated wholesale — not only in Staffordshire but also in Scottish potteries and elsewhere. However, George Hood, whose pottery was at Bourne's Bank, made many of the attractive dogs and another dog and animal figure maker was James Dudson of Han-

ley. John and Rebecca Lloyd marked their products LLOYD, SHELTON, impressed underneath or at the back. Other potters known to have made figures of this type were Burton (Stoke), Baggaley (Hanley), Machin (Hanley), and Massey, Walley, Booth and William and Jane Beech, all of Burslem.

The best known and documented potter who specialised in chimney ornament figures was Sampson Smith (1813-78). He began work in Longton in about 1846. The discovery of some of his original moulds shows that he was responsible at least for figures of Moody, the revivalist preacher, Wellington, Burns and his Mary, Fred Archer the jockey, and a series of dogs.

In the survey which follows the name in small capitals is the title found on the figure.

Robert Burns and Highland Mary. One of the models known to have been made by Sampson Smith. Reproductions were made from the original press-mould until recently.

LEFT: *The Prince of Wales with one of his dogs, about 1862. It is likely that this figure was produced when the first rumours of his marriage were circulating.*
RIGHT: *Empress Eugenie and the Prince Imperial, about 1856. The attribution is confirmed by an identical figure inscribed in black script 'Empress Eugenie'.*

ROYALTY

The largest single group of nineteenth-century figures is made up of the British royal family and its immediate connections. Queen Victoria and Prince Albert had four sons and five daughters, most of whom were modelled at least twice.

There is a very wide selection of figures of the Queen, alone or with Albert or one of the children. Some are untitled, and some are labelled VICTORIA or QUEEN or occasionally QUEEN OF ENGLAND. Most are recognisable by her demeanour, dress or crown. Prince ALBERT appears in several forms, singly or with Victoria or a child. The earliest figure probably dates from about 1840. An untitled figure can often be identified by the pencil moustache.

The PRINCE OF WALES (also PRINCE), born in 1841, was modelled several times. Individual figures show him standing, in civilian clothes, in uniform and in Highland dress, and on horseback. After his engagement to Princess Alexandra of Denmark pairs of figures were made entitled PRINCE and PRINCESS singly or in one model. Such pairs were made for most royal marriages. Princess Victoria (PRINCESS ROYAL), born in 1840, also appears, untitled, in attractive childhood groups and childhood models of Prince ALFRED always showed him in sailor's clothes. There are models of all but three of the other children (and their spouses).

A Crimean War triple group. It was made about 1854. The figures depict the three sovereigns: Sultan Abd-ul-Medjid, Queen Victoria and Napoleon III.

SOLDIERS AND SAILORS

THE CRIMEAN WAR, 1854-6

Between the battle of Waterloo in 1815 and the First World War, Britain was involved in a number of localised, remote wars. In 1853 Russia invaded Turkey, and France and Sardinia joined Britain in the fight to defeat her, attacking the Russian base at Sebastopol in the Crimea.

Staffordshire potters had plenty of subjects. Among the allied sovereigns is a double figure of Queen Victoria and Napoleon III of France (unmistakable with his moustache), labelled QUEEN EMPEROR, as well as several single figures of the Emperor (LOUIS NAPOLEON) and his Empress Eugenie (EMPRESS OF FRANCE). Three sovereigns appear in groups labelled THE ALLIED POWERS or TURKEY-ENGLAND-FRANCE. The SULTAN of Turkey is represented, as is VICTOR EMMANUEL (also KING OF SARDINIA).

Many prominent military figures are represented, including the Turkish commander-in-chief, OMAR PASHA (OMER PACHA) and three French generals. There are also one or two representative groups such as ENGLAND AND FRANCE, VIVAN-DIERE (a woman standing in front of a mounted French soldier) and a double group of Turkish soldiers in fezes, untitled.

Three British naval officers appear, but the interest was in the army. Probably the best known military figure was Field Marshal LORD RAGLAN (also FM RAGLAN, RAGLAN and L RAGLAN), who commanded the army until his death in July 1855. At least five different figures of him were made. He was succeeded by General Sir James Simpson (GNL SIMPSON and SIR JAMES SIMPSON), commemorated in at least three figures, in one with a mound of flags, guns and shells against his right leg. A pair to this is a similar model of General Sir Charles WINDHAM. Other commanders are recorded as well as figures from heroic incidents, but the most famous figure produced by the war was Florence Nightingale (see cover).

There are several models of the Russian fortress of SEBASTOPOL and a number of patriotic figures and groups including BRITAIN'S GLORY, SCOTLAND'S PRIDE, THE WOUNDED SOLDIER, THE SOLDIER'S FAREWELL, THE SOLDIER'S RETURN, BEGGING SAILOR, READY AND WILLING and a number of untitled heroic groups.

THE INDIAN MUTINY, 1857-9

The Commander-in-Chief in India was General SIR COLIN CAMPBELL (also CAMPBELL, COLIN CAMPBELL), of whom at least six figures are known, most with a Scottish bonnet or trews, and the most successful military commander was General Sir Henry Havelock (MG HAVELOCK KCB, HAVELOCK, G HAVELOCK, SIR S H HAVELOCK), who recaptured Cawnpore and twice relieved Lucknow. Several

models were made of him.

The Mutiny also produced the first genuine folk hero recorded in a Staffordshire figure, HIGHLAND JESSIE, wife of a corporal at the siege of Lucknow in 1857. She inspired the garrison to hold out by shrieking that she could hear the approaching pipes of the relieving column. She is shown holding a rifle in her hand, supporting a wounded soldier, and standing with a soldier sitting on her right.

THE FRANCO-PRUSSIAN WAR, 1870

The Franco-Prussian War was the turning point in Anglo-French relationships. At the end of a very short campaign France was defeated by an obviously powerful Prussia. The KING OF PRUSSIA, William I (who became Emperor of Germany the following year), was modelled in two versions but only one model is known of the man who engineered the

LEFT: *Admiral Sir Charles Napier, commander of the Baltic Fleet during the Crimean War. Figures of Napier were modelled to pair with Admiral Sir James Dundas.*
RIGHT: *Field Marshal Lord Raglan and Sir Colin Campbell, two of the best known military figures in the Crimean War.*

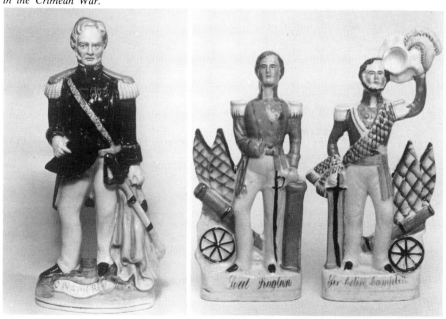

ABOVE: *A pair representing the British lion sitting upon Napoleon III at the time of the Anglo-French war scare, about 1860.*

LEFT: *Sir John Franklin died looking for the North-West Passage in 1847. Lady Franklin refused to believe that her husband was dead until irrefutable evidence was discovered in 1857. Up to that date she had despatched five separate expedition ships, at her own expense, to search for the lost explorers.*

LEFT: *A well modelled figure of Garibaldi, the liberator of Italy, based on an engraving from the 'Illustrated London News' of January 1861.*
RIGHT: *Abraham Lincoln. This figure was probably issued in 1861 after Lincoln was elected President of the United States and gave his famous anti-slavery speech which was to lead to the Civil War.*

war, said to be the most powerful man in Europe at the time, Bismarck. The figure (titled and misspelt G BISMARK) shows the Chancellor of Prussia in uniform on horseback. A pair to this is a figure of the Prussian commander responsible for the rapid defeat of France, Count von Moltke (G MOLTKE). There are other Prussian figures but only two French commanders, Marshal MacMahon (MAC MAHON) and Marshal BAZAINE.

THE LIBERATION OF ITALY, 1870

The triumphant march to Rome of Garibaldi and his handful of red-shirted followers caught the imagination of the British people. At least thirteen figures of Garibaldi were made, most of them titled simply GARIBALDI but also GARIBALDI AT WAR, GARIBALDI AT HOME and LIBERTE. Colonel Peard (C PEARD), Garibaldi's English right-hand man, also appears, with Garibaldi (on a watch holder) and singly.

THE AMERICAN CIVIL WAR, 1861-5

This war aroused public sympathy not least because of Harriet Beecher Stowe's book *Uncle Tom's Cabin*, published nine years before the start of the war. Many figures and groups were made of characters from the book, including UNCLE TOM, AUNT CHLOE, EVA & UNCLE TOM, TOPSY & EVA and GEORGE & ELIZA HARRIS.

THE EGYPTIAN AND SUDAN CAMPAIGNS, 1882-98

In 1882 the Egyptian army mutinied as the Indian Army had in 1857. This rebellion was crushed by the popular Sir Garnet Wolseley (SIR G WOLSELEY, G WOLSELEY, WOLSELEY) who also commanded the expedition sent too late to relieve GENERAL GORDON (also GORDON, G GORDON) besieged by the Mahdi in Khartoum. General Gordon was killed a few days before relief arrived.

Other figures from the Sudan campaign were of Major General Sir Herbert Stewart (G STEWART), who commanded the Khartoum relief column and was killed in the fighting, paired with Colonel Frederick Gustavus Burnaby (C BUR-

ABOVE LEFT: *John Brown, the American abolitionist. Two years before the beginning of the Civil War, he led an attack on the arsenal at Harper's Ferry, was captured and hanged. The incident gave rise to the famous song 'John Brown's Body'.*
ABOVE RIGHT: *General Sir Garnet Wolseley, the popular commander-in-chief who led the expedition to relieve General Gordon at Khartoum in 1884-5.*
BELOW: *Two figures of General Gordon, Governor-General of the Sudan, whose murder in Khartoum in 1885 caused a public outcry.*

NABY), who was famous for his ride through the middle of Russian Asia from Kazala to Khiva in 1875.

The River War of 1896-8 was fought against the Mahdi's followers in Egypt. The two personalities commemorated were LORD KITCHENER (also KITCHENER, THE SIRDAR), and Major General Sir HECTOR MACDONALD (also MAJOR MACDONALD, MACDONALD), 'Fighting Mac', who, unusually, had risen from the ranks and led the victory at Omdurman.

THE BOER WAR, 1899-1902

This bitter war showed the problems of recording people too soon after the event in a medium as permanent as pottery. For example, SIR REDVERS BULLER (also BULLER) was Commander-in-Chief in South Africa for only three months before he was sacked and sent home. LORD ROBERTS (also ROBERTS) and Sir John French (GEN FRENCH, FRENCH) were modelled but the best known figure from the war was Colonel RSS BADEN POWELL, who commanded the garrison of Mafeking while it was under siege during 1899-1900. Three models were made, all wearing the famous slouch hat.

The Boer War was the last military event commemorated by Staffordshire figures in this form. By 1914 tastes had changed and the crudely modelled flatback figure was no more.

PREACHERS AND PRELATES

With few known exceptions, all the religious figures made in Staffordshire during the nineteenth century refer to nonconformists: they represented popular taste, which was against the established church. A number of historic religious figures were made, probably about 1850, and the first group of five anti-Catholic figures dates from 1851, when there was a fervent anti-Popery outcry. These pre-Victorian subjects include ARCHBISHOP CRANMER, who was burnt at the stake for heresy in 1556. The model represents the scene, and below the title is written BURNT AT OXFORD MARCH 21ST 1556. Two other well known Protestant martyrs were Bishops RIDLEY and LATIMER.

A figure of a Catholic priest with his left hand resting on a scroll bearing a pro-Catholic quotation is paired with PROTESTANTISM, the figure of a young girl with her right hand on a scroll bearing quotations from the Bible. The last of the anti-Popery figures, made in about 1851, carries no title but shows two figures, a girl holding a bag labelled £10,000 and a

The two Protestant martyrs, Bishops Ridley and Latimer, burnt at the stake together in 1555. Under the title are written the famous words of Latimer, 'Be of good comfort, Master Ridley, and play the man: we shall this day light such a candle, by God's grace, in England, as I trust shall never be put out'.

15

LEFT: *John Wesley preaching from the pulpit.*
RIGHT: *Moody and Sankey, the American evangelist preachers. The figures, made by Sampson Smith, probably commemorate their first visit to England in 1873. The original mould for Moody was found in 1948 and a number of reproductions cast from it.*

kneeling priest holding out a veil towards her.

Several figures were made of John WESLEY, the most famous of the eighteenth-century nonconformist preachers, who died in 1791. Two versions show him preaching from a pulpit and another figure shows him in ecclesiastical dress, holding an open Bible in his hands.

Other notable characters include the Baptist preacher the REVEREND CHRISTMAS EVANS, a fiery Christian, blind in his right eye. His figure shows the right eye unmistakably closed. A famous Victorian Quaker and philanthropist was Joseph John Gurney (J J GURNEY), whose figure shows him standing in a cut-away coat and flowered waistcoat. Another probable pair, and the earliest proper Catholic Staffordshire figures, are figures of Pope Pius IX (HIS HOLINESS THE POPE), who was Pope from 1846 to 1878, and CARDINAL MANNING, who became Archbishop of

Westminster in 1865 and a cardinal in 1875. Two pairs of untitled figures, 3 inches (75 mm) high, of a friar and a nun have been identified as Sister Margaret Mary Hallahan, who founded several Dominican communities in the Midlands between 1846 and 1853, and Père Bernard Moulaert, who worked with her.

The founder of the Salvation Army, General Booth, was commemorated in an unusual, untitled bust, coloured in dark blue and brick red. He wears a peaked cap on which the words 'Salvation Army' are written, and a red jersey under his blue uniform, carrying a device with the words 'Blood and Fire'. There are at least three designs of the Reverend Charles Spurgeon (C H SPURGEON), a Baptist preacher who for over thirty years from 1861 drew large congregations to the Metropolitan Tabernacle whenever he preached there.

ABOVE: *Dick Turpin, the highway-man, and Tom King, Turpin's companion in crime, made about 1851. These eighteenth-century characters were depicted in a number of different models including these made by Sampson Smith.*

RIGHT: *William Corder and Maria Marten, his victim of the murder in the Red Barn in 1828.*

17

James Rush of Potash Farm, and his mistress Emily Sandford, whose evidence convicted him. Rush stands with a scroll (probably the draft of his fourteen-hour speech for his defence at the trial).

VILLAINS AND VICTIMS

It is an indication of how important Staffordshire figures were as recorders of news and mementoes of important events that not a few villains, their victims and even the places where the crimes were committed were modelled.

Although he was hanged in 1739, DICK TURPIN, the highwayman, was still familiar enough to be modelled as a Staffordshire portrait figure. Less familiar today is TOM KING his companion, modelled in as many variants as Dick Turpin, the two usually being done in pairs. They owed their fame to Harrison Ainsworth's novel *Rookwood* published in 1834.

Also outside the chronological range is the murder in the Red Barn (1828). Among the commemorative pieces made are various models of the barn itself, where William Corder murdered and buried Maria Marten and her child, and figures of Corder and Maria. These groups seem to have been taken from engravings that appeared in the contemporary record of the murder and the trial.

More complicated and grisly was the case in 1848 of James Blomfield Rush (JAMES B RUSH) of Potash Farm, who murdered his creditor, Isaac Jermy, and his son, and wounded two other people. A large number of different Staffordshire figures of the events were produced, including Rush himself, paired with EMILY SANDFORD, whose evidence was largely responsible for his conviction, and labelled models of Stanfield Hall, the home of Isaac Jermy, Potash Farm and even of Norwich Castle, where Rush was hanged.

In the course of two years Doctor WILLIAM PALMER poisoned his wife, his brother and his friend John Parsons Cook. His figure shows him standing, looking both benign and intelligent. A

18

model of the house in Rugeley, Stafford-shire, where the murders were committed is entitled PALMER'S HOUSE.

The case of the Tichborne Claimant was probably the most celebrated civil action of the Victorian era. Arthur Orton convinced Lady Tichborne, widow of the tenth Baronet, that he was her long-lost eldest son and therefore the heir to the title. He brought a suit in the courts to deprive the five-year-old twelfth Baronet of the title, in his own favour. After nearly three months the court decided that he was an imposter and he was arrested for perjury. He was finally sentenced to fourteen years in prison. The figure (SIR R TICHBORNE), though portly, does not show his enormous size.

Frank Gardiner was the Australian counterpart of Dick Turpin, and his model is a pair with one of Turpin. Gardiner was a bush ranger and in 1862 he and his gang held up a gold consignment in New South Wales. Eventually he was sent to prison for thirty-two years.

RIGHT: *Arthur Orton, the 'Tichborne Claimant'. After a long trial, he was found guilty of perjury and served fourteen years in prison. Moderately portly though the figure is, it does not do justice to his true size.*

BELOW: *Potash Farm (left), the property which caused James Rush to murder Isaac Jermy and his son in 1848; and Stanfield Hall (right), Isaac Jermy's home, where the double murder took place.*

19

An unidentified batsman, made about 1865. This is probably Julius Caesar, a celebrated batsman and a member of the All England eleven from 1849 to 1867.

Master M'Grath and Pretender, made about 1871; two of the most famous coursing greyhounds of the nineteenth century.

SPORT

One of the most evocative Staffordshire portrait groups is the one entitled HEENAN SAYERS, showing a pair of boxers in breeches, each with a left fist connecting with his opponent's face. The group commemorates one of the last bare-fist fights, fought between Carmel Heenan, a famous American heavyweight, and Tom Sayers, champion of England, in 1860. Tom Cribb, champion of England from 1809 to 1824, defeated Tom Molyneux, a black American, in 1810 and 1811. They were modelled by Enoch Wood and these figures are rare and much sought after. Both figures are shown wearing yellow knee breeches and pink stockings, standing on grassy mounds in a fighting attitude.

There are several figures of cricketers but none of them are titled: the attributions to particular cricketers are from other contemporary evidence. They are rare and expensive. Fuller Pilch, who played for Kent between 1836 and 1854 and was regarded as the best batsman of the time, and Thomas Box, the finest wicket-keeper, appear on a pair of spill vases, the one taking guard and the other crouched. A pair believed to show George Parr, captain of All England about 1857, and Julius Caesar, a great All England batsman, shows Parr with a cricket ball in his right hand, a cricket bat of the old spoon shape leaning against a wicket and Caesar at the wicket. Frederick William Lillywhite was the first exponent of the round-arm style of bowling and the most famous bowler of his generation. His figure shows him in top hat and trousers supported by braces, the ball in his right hand.

A figure of the champion jockey Fred Archer (CHAMPION JOCKEY), made about 1875, shows him mounted on an unknown brown horse and wearing yellow and green silks. He rode 2,447 winners. This may be the only horse-racing figure. Greyhound racing is represented by two outstanding greyhounds, Master M'Grath (M'GRATH), a black dog, probably the most famous ever raced and even bidden to meet Queen Victoria, and a tawny dog called PRETENDER, a rival of M'Grath.

21

*The Duke of Welling-
ton on Copenhagen,
the chestnut horse he
rode at Waterloo. Re-
productions of this
model incorrectly col-
our the horse cream.*

POLITICIANS

Most of the important politicians of the Victorian era were modelled. The Duke of WELLINGTON, who made his name and earned his dukedom as a brilliant general, is commemorated equally for his career in politics. There are many figures, the earlier ones uniformed and often equestrian, sometimes untitled. Later figures show him in civilian dress, except for the figure IN MEMORY OF THE DUKE OF WELLINGTON, modelled after his death, where he is in uniform again.

Irish affairs were prominent for most of the nineteenth century and among the chief protagonists of Home Rule appear Daniel O'Connell MP (D O'CONNEL, DAN O'CONNELL), in 1830 the first Irish Catholic MP, and Charles Stewart Parnell MP (C S PARNELL), who persuaded the Prime Minister, Gladstone, to support the cause. In one figure Parnell is shown dressed as a gladiator with a large club in his left hand and a flag in his right bearing the Union Jack and the Irish harp.

SIR ROBERT PEEL (also PEEL, SIR R PEEL, S R PEEL) was popular with the

22

Sir Robert Peel was a favourite character with the public because of his repeal of the Corn Laws in 1846. As a result, a considerable number of figures were made by the potters. Most show him standing, holding a speech or scroll which in some versions is marked 'Repeal of the Corn Law'. This figure is based on the engraving which appeared in the 'Illustrated London News' on 6th July 1850, four days after his death in Hyde Park in a riding accident.

public because he repealed the hated Corn Laws. At least eight figures are known. Most show him standing holding a speech or scroll and in two he is on horseback. The chief architects of the repeal were Richard Cobden (R COBDEN) and John Bright. Bright does not appear to have been modelled but there are at least two figures of Cobden, in one of which he is shown sitting with a scroll in his right hand and by his leg a cornucopia pouring forth the fruits of the earth.

Most models of William Ewart Gladstone (MR GLADSTONE, GLADSTONE, W E GLADSTONE) show him standing in formal frock-coat with a speech in one hand, but one version shows him in belligerent pose with an axe in one hand and a flag above his shoulder, and in another he is standing in a pulpit, beating the head of a turbaned Turk below. This was made in the 1870s when Turkish repression of subject nations had aroused great indignation. It is labelled TURKISH EXTINGUISHER. Alternating with Gladstone as prime minister, until his death in 1881, was Benjamin Disraeli, created Earl of Beaconsfield in 1876. Two figures are known, both pairs to figures of Gladstone, labelled BEACONSFIELD.

ABOVE: *Grace Darling and her father, 1838. The model shows a graphic representation of the scene when the Darlings rowed through stormy seas to rescue five people stranded on rocks near the Farne Islands.*

LEFT: *'Bloomers', made about 1851. One of many figures showing the remarkable new outfit of Turkish trousers and knee-length dress introduced by the American Mrs Amelia Bloomer in 1849. This figure is probably based on Rebecca Isaacs, who sang the song 'I want to be a Bloomer!' in the music halls of the time.*

24

The Lion Slayer and Will Watch. These large flamboyant figures illustrate the nineteenth-century cottagers' craving for the colourful and heroic. The Sampson Smith figure of the Lion Slayer of about 1854 (left) is a portrait of the big-game hunter Roualeyn George Gordon-Cumming whereas Will Watch (right) was a fictional swashbuckler and the hero of several popular melodramas.

HEROES AND HEROINES

James BRAIDWOOD was for nearly thirty years superintendent of the London Fire-engine Establishment. He was killed on duty in 1861 during the great fire in Tooley Street. London came to a standstill for his funeral.

The flamboyant Shah of Persia, Nasr-ed-Din, visited England in 1873. He became one of the sights of London and his gaily attired equestrian model bears the first line of the music-hall song HAVE YOU SEEN THE SHAH?

Mrs Amelia Bloomer (BLOOMERS) of New York was a pioneer of the women's rights movement. In 1849 she invented and wore a new style of dress which combined a short skirt and a pair of long baggy trousers, caught in at the ankles. The Victorians were not ready for such audacity and bloomers became a huge joke on both sides of the Atlantic.

Roualeyn George Gordon-Cumming was one of the first of the celebrated big-game hunters. His book, *Five Years of a Hunter's Life in the Far Interior of Africa,* was an immediate success and in 1851 he showed his lion skins and other trophies on a special stand at the Great Exhibition. Two figures of him are known, one untitled and the other labelled THE LION SLAYER.

In Hungary in 1848 an unsuccessful rising was led by Louis KOSSUTH, who was forced to flee for his life. He came to England in 1851 and was received as a patriot and a hero. He is an unmistakably central European character, with plumed Tyrolean hat and flamboyantly cut coat.

Jenny Jones and Edward Morgan became folk heroes when their romance attracted the attention of Charles James Mathews, whose song about them, written in 1836, remained popular for twenty years. Jenny Jones was a dairymaid at Pontblyddin Farm near Llangollen, where Edward (known as Ned) Morgan was a ploughman; he had returned after twenty years in the Navy to marry Jenny, who had waited for him. The three figures are all based on contemporary lithographs.

AUTHORS AND ACTORS

Most of the writers modelled as Staffordshire figures during the Victorian era were not contemporary personalities. There are several models of Shakespeare and of his house and many versions of Robert Burns, sometimes with Highland Mary. Figures of Milton, Chaucer, Pope, Matthew Prior, Byron, Rousseau and Voltaire are all known. The first contemporary literary figure is SIR WALTER SCOTT (also S W SCOTT). There are two quite different figures of him, both pairs to similar figures of Robert Burns, and made in the 1880s.

Elizabeth Landon, who died at the age of thirty-six in 1838, was a very popular poetess and novelist. The Staffordshire figure is taken from the frontispiece of a collected edition of her poems. It shows her sitting on a sofa, with a book on her lap.

Two very similar versions are known of Eliza Cook, the only strictly contempor-

ary poet to be recorded as a Staffordshire figure. She is standing, with long ringlets down to her shoulder, dressed in a checked bodice and flounced skirt, holding a book or scroll in her right hand.

Actors were better known and modelled more often. The fashion was to model serious actors and actresses in their most celebrated roles. William Charles Macready, whose most famous role was Richard III, was modelled in that role (labelled MACREADY), as Macbeth (titled MACBETH) and as Shylock (titled SHYLOCK).

A figure entitled LADY MACBETH, which is a pair to the Macready figure, is of Isabella Glyn and is taken from a contemporary engraving of the well known Shakespearean actress, who played opposite Macready on many occasions.

There are two interesting double groups of Shakespearean actors and actresses. WINTER'S TALE, showing Florizel and Perdita, portrays Frederick Robinson and Jenny Marston, who played these parts at Sadler's Wells in 1851. The other group shows Charlotte and Susan Cushman, two Boston sisters who became extremely popular as Romeo and Juliet in 1845. The group is labelled on the base O THINK'ST THOU WE SHALL EVER MEET AGAIN?

In 1861 Edward Askew Sothern played Lord Dundreary, described as a 'brainless peer', in *Our American Cousin* by Tom Taylor. This play was enormously popular for twenty years. The figure, untitled, shows Sothern in a very long frock-coat and with a monocle, long hair and whiskers. 'Dundreary whiskers' be-

came a popular fashion.

Other figures of earlier actors include David Garrick as Richard III and John Philip Kemble as Hamlet. The celebrated Mrs Siddons was also modelled as Lady Macbeth.

Victorian musicians were poorly served by Staffordshire potters. The most famous singer commemorated, and the favourite, was JENNY LIND (also M LIND), the 'Swedish Nightingale'. She first appeared on the London stage in 1847 as Alice in Meyerbeer's opera *Robert Le Diable*. Another favourite role was Maria in *La Figlia del Reggimento* by Donizetti. Many figures of her were made in these and other roles and as simple portraits.

One impresario responsible for Jenny

LEFT: *Sir Walter Scott and Maida. This figure, together with the companion figure of Robert Burns, was almost certainly made during the 1880s.*
RIGHT: *The actor William Charles Macready in the role of Rob Roy Macgregor. His dramatic stance is based on a titled tinsel picture published by A. Park in 1840.*

Lind's appearances was Louis Antoine Jullien (JULLIEN), a French conductor, who had a great success with the musical public during the 1840s and 1850s. His figures show him in a typical attitude — perfectly dressed, his neatly bearded face uplifted and staring proudly into the distance, his music score open in his left hand.

There is a fine selection of figures related to the circus. Outstanding is POLITO'S MENAGERIE, made about 1830, a model on six legs of a booth at a fair.

The most famous elephant ever was JUMBO, reputed to be the largest elephant ever seen. Between 1861 and 1881 Jumbo was one of the main attractions at the Regent's Park Zoo, until he was sold to the American Phineas T. Barnum. Un-happily the elephant, having earned Barnum colossal sums of money, one day charged a stationary railway engine. Both had to be destroyed.

The most famous lion tamer of the time was the American Isaac van Amburgh, who first came in 1839 to the Drury Lane Theatre with an act including a cage full of lions, leopards and a lamb. Queen Victoria loved him, going to his performances three times within a fortnight. At least two models of him were made. The best known, labelled MR VAN AMBURGH, shows him standing dressed as a Roman gladiator, his right hand resting on the head of a lion, his left on a tiger and with what is probably a lamb at his feet: a leopard clings to his back and peers over his shoulder.

Mazeppa on a horse, about 1864. The American actress Adah Isaacs Menken had a sensational success at Astley's Circus when she appeared, apparently nude, in a story based on a wild ride across seventeenth-century Russia.

Jumbo, reputed by the famous showman Barnum to be the largest elephant ever seen. He was so popular with the British public that songs were composed about him and several different models made by the potters.

ABOVE: *Miniature figures. A wide range of subjects was made including members of the royal family, Nurse Cavell, political and military figures such as Havelock (left), height 5 inches (127 mm), and the unidentified clown (right), height 4¼ inches (108 mm). The fact that the clown's head is a whistle lends support to the theory that some at least of these miniatures were intended as toys.*

LEFT: *St George and the Dragon. A small highly coloured version of England's patron saint. Many different models were made of St George to cater for nineteenth-century patriotism.*

A number of clues on these figures have not helped to identify them. The girl on the left might be an actress or dancer, the dove in her hand being a guide to her character. The parrot and performing dog accompanying the kilted male dancer (right) suggest a circus or fair. The heroic central figure (height 17½ inches, 445 mm) is listed as an unidentified forester; the title in gilt script, OR, adds to the mystery.

COLLECTING STAFFORDSHIRE FIGURES

A would-be collector should familiarise himself with the range and variety by seeing as many figures as possible in shops and museums. The major auction houses regularly include Staffordshire figures in their sales; these provide an ideal opportunity for the collector to handle items and become aware of current prices. Damaged pieces should not be bought unless they are very cheap and fill a particular gap in the collection.

Staffordshire figures have been reproduced, often from the original moulds, since late Victorian times. Like the originals, these reproductions show the normal signs of age, such as chips, crazing and rubbed gilding. In such cases colouring can be a helpful guide to both dating and faking. For example, the vivid underglaze cobalt blue much used for uniforms until about 1860 was then virtually discontinued: conversely, any figure decorated with a crude iron red is likely to be a modern one. Gilding, too, is an important aid to dating. In the 1850s a new liquid form of gold was introduced which no longer required the labour-intensive hand finishing. This new harsh-coloured gilt compares unfavourably with the gentle soft colour of burnished gold.

FURTHER READING

Balston, Thomas. *Staffordshire Portrait Figures of the Victorian Age*. Faber, 1958.
Balston, Thomas. *Supplement to Staffordshire Portrait Figures*. John Hall, 1963.
Haggar, R. G. *Staffordshire Chimney Ornaments*. Phoenix House, 1955.
Hall, John. *Staffordshire Portrait Figures*. Letts, 1972.
Pugh, P. D. Gordon. *Staffordshire Portrait Figures and Allied Subjects of the Victorian Era*. Barrie and Jenkins, 1981.

PLACES TO VISIT

In addition to more general collections, some of the places listed here have figures relating to one particular person and these are indicated accordingly. Intending visitors are advised to find out the times of opening before making a special journey.

Ashmolean Museum of Art and Archaeology, Beaumont Street, Oxford OX1 2PH. Telephone: Oxford (0865) 512651.
Bantock House, Bantock Park, Merridale Road, Wolverhampton, West Midlands WV3 9LQ. Telephone: Wolverhampton (0902) 24548. (The Balston Collection.)
The Brighton Museum and Art Gallery, Church Street, Brighton, East Sussex. Telephone: Brighton (0273) 603005. (The Willett Collection.)
Disraeli Museum, Hughenden Manor, High Wycombe, Buckinghamshire. Telephone: High Wycombe (0494) 32580. (Benjamin Disraeli, Earl of Beaconsfield.)
Fitzwilliam Museum, Trumpington Street, Cambridge CB2 1RB. Telephone: Cambridge (0223) 69501.
Nelson Collection and Local History Centre, Priory Street, Monmouth, Gwent. Telephone: Monmouth (0600) 3519. (Lord Nelson.)
Scunthorpe Borough Museum and Art Gallery, Oswald Road, Scunthorpe, South Humberside DN15 7BD. Telephone: Scunthorpe (0724) 843533. (John Wesley.)
Stoke-on-Trent City Museum and Art Gallery, Bethesda Street, Hanley, Stoke-on-Trent, Staffordshire ST1 3DW. Telephone: Stoke-on-Trent (0782) 273173.
Stratfield Saye House, near Reading, Berkshire RG7 2BT. Telephone: Basingstoke (0256) 882882. (Duke of Wellington.)
Victoria and Albert Museum, Cromwell Road, South Kensington, London SW7 2RL. Telephone: 01-589 6371.
York Castle Museum, Tower Street, York. Telephone: York (0904) 53611.